D0848749

Golf: The Art of the Mental Game
100 Classic Golf Tips

Golf: Th
the Ment

100 Classi

e Art of
al Game

Golf Tips

Dr. Joseph Parent

Drawing by

Anthony Ravielli

Foreword by Tom Watson

Based on the Bestseller ZEN

Conte

6
FOREWORD – TOM WATSON

10
IDEAL ATTITUDES

34
MENTAL OBSTACLES

70
PRACTICE AND PREPARATION

100
COURSE STRATEGY

134
GOLFING YOUR BALL

166
GETTING OUT OF TROUBLE

192
HOLING OUT

nts

THROUGHOUT MY YEARS walking the fairways of the world, golf has afforded me the opportunity to make many friends I might never have had, and to witness genius both on and off the course.

One of the people whom I was privileged to meet along the way was Anthony Ravielli. A small man with Coke-bottle glasses and plaid shirts, Tony—as his friends called him—became a dear friend and my artistic curator. Over fifteen years of working together, from the early 1980s into the mid-1990s, I came to know Tony's work. A tireless artist and a stickler for details, Tony delivered his best in each illustration.

When Ben Hogan decided to analyze the swing, put it into words, and create the visual document, he sought out Tony. Admiring Tony's work for both *Sports Illustrated* and *Golf Digest*, Hogan created the perfect recipe, including the words of Herbert Warren Wind and what would soon become the most recognized golf-instruction illustrations ever created.

So when it came time to put together the team for *Getting Up and Down: How to Save Strokes from Forty Yards and In*, after my 1982 U.S. Open win at Pebble Beach, there was no doubt whom to go to for illustrations.

Developing good technique based on the fundamentals that the Ravielli illustrations walk the golfer through is essential. Through his unparalleled knowledge of anatomy, Tony was able to capture the nuances of the swing. While technology may reduce distance or perhaps lessen the degree of an imperfect shot, there is no way to become a good golfer other than to practice, and to do so with an understanding of the requirements of each shot.

When Christopher Obetz asked me to write this foreword, I was delighted to know that once again golf's vaults of one-of-a-kind Ravielli drawings would be opened for all to enjoy and learn from.

All of us who have known and worked with Tony sincerely appreciate his talent and the precision of his illustrations. Not only a premier artist, his passion and good will made anyone who worked with him a friend. We all miss you Tony.

Wishing you all the best on and off the course,

Tom Watson

SOMETHING ANTHONY RAVIELLI understood
and tried to convey in his drawings is that technical
proficiency alone isn't enough to make a great golfer.
Players of all levels have long been aware of the impact
that thoughts and emotions can have on one's game.
The confidence of champions has always been recognized as a factor vital to their success, and any kind of
breakdown symbolic of their failure.

Golf: The Art of the Mental Game unites
Ravielli's exceptional technical hand with one of the
most distinguished voices in mental game coaching.
Dr. Joseph Parent for many years has been teaching the
world's best golfers how to turn their minds into allies
instead of enemies, helping them to get out of their own
way and make the most of their abilities. Whatever a
player's level of technical ability, approaching the game
with an ideal attitude and understanding how to over-
come mental obstacles can make all the difference in
how much someone enjoys a round of golf—let alone
how well he or she plays it.

With this book, each and every player can learn
to become a better golfer and gain a better understanding of the influence one's mind can have on the physical
actions and reactions of life. It's a tribute to Anthony
Ravielli that his work lives on to inspire future genera-
tions of golfers; and it's a tribute to Dr. Joseph Parent
that his ideas are so perfectly complemented by such
timeless illustrations of golfers in action.

Christopher Obetz

100 TIPS

"I don't hit every green.
I don't birdie every hole.
I don't win every tournament.
But I believe I will."

Tiger Woods

Ideal Att

itudes

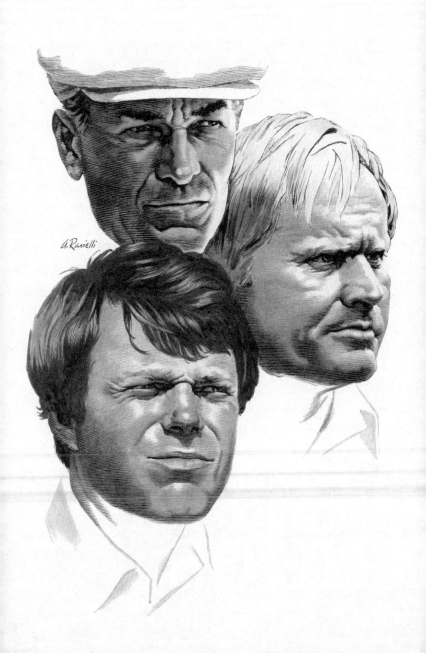

01

THE MENTAL GAME OF CHAMPIONS

What sets champions apart from the also-rans is the mental game. The cornerstone of the mental strength of champions is confidence. This is not a temporary, conditional confidence that disappears when they are not playing well. They believe in themselves and their abilities regardless of the circumstances: their confidence is unconditional.

Unconditional confidence requires a broad perspective, independent of moment-to-moment results. The wider the perspective we have, the better we can weather the ups and downs within a round, a tournament, or a season. We can handle difficulties with poise and we can accept successes with humility. Being fearless in the moment is the expression of that true confidence.

When you're struggling with your swing or your short game, reflect on the times you've played your best. Know that you never lose your abilities; they just get covered up—usually by too many complications. Go back to some simple keys for your swing and your putting stroke. Never stop believing in yourself, and you'll find your way back to playing your best.

02

BEING IN THE ZONE

Being in the zone means playing golf with total freedom from doubt and self-consciousness. It doesn't mean you'll hit every shot perfectly, but even a missed shot here or there won't diminish your confidence.

How do we achieve that freedom? It starts with training that requires some conscious intention to groove the most efficient habits in the setup and swing. Consciously thinking about technique is something that should only be done in practice, while you're learning. When you take your game to the course, you need to trust yourself to make the best swing you can. In playing the game, self-consciously thinking about how to swing while you're swinging gets in the way more than it helps.

Trusting your swing doesn't mean that you'll make a great swing every time. It means you'll let your body do its best to reproduce the feel and tempo you've ingrained on the range.

When it's time to swing, let your mind be filled with an image of the target and let your body swing the club without self-consciously thinking about how to do it. That is being in the zone.

A. Ravielli

03

PROCESS OVER RESULT

Thinking too much about the result you want from a shot can get in the way of executing it properly. It can make you tight with tension or excited with anticipation. Either way, it means interference with the flow of your routine and your swing. A better approach is to focus entirely on the following four-step process:

1. Choose a target that will leave you in the position you want without too much risk of landing in trouble.
2. Have a good image of the shot you want to play to that target.
3. Feel the swing you want to make to produce that image.
4. Commit to that swing. Keep a smooth flow through your routine and address, and a good tempo through your swing.

Take care of the process in that way and the results will take care of themselves.

04 PRE-ACCEPTANCE

The greatest interference to swinging freely is the fear of an unwanted result. Being willing to accept whatever result a shot may produce, and feeling that you can handle whatever the future holds, remove the interference that comes with fear. To remove this interference, you need to be willing to accept whatever result a shot may produce, and be ready for whatever is required on the next shot.

Pre-acceptance of the outcome is important because golf is a game of percentages. The less chance you think you have of executing a shot successfully, the more difficult it will be to make a free swing.

Ben Hogan once said that he considered it a good round of golf if he hit just three shots exactly the way he wanted. He understood that golf is more a game of misses than it is a game of perfection. That's why top professionals say that they often win tournaments in which they make better misses. You can score very well with good misses. But your misses won't be very good ones if you don't commit to your shots.

Before you set up to the ball, do your best to be optimistic and committed to your shot while also being realistic about the range of possible results. With that mind-set you will find yourself hitting better shots, even when they don't come out perfectly.

05

EXCITEMENT OR ANXIETY?

If you're in contention in a big match or tournament, you'll undoubtedly feel some form of nervousness. It's the result of a natural flow of adrenaline that is released when anyone faces a challenging situation. There are two different ways you can interpret that feeling: as excitement or as anxiety.

Even the greatest of champions feels nervous on the first tee of the last round when they are in contention. They interpret it as excitement. They want to feel that way because it means they are in the hunt for the trophy and ready for the challenge of competition.

Less experienced golfers take the nervous feeling to mean that they are in danger of failing, and play from a fearful mindset that rarely succeeds.

By recognizing your nervous feeling as excitement about your chances of winning, rather than as anxiety over the fear of losing, you can make a conscious choice to interpret the feeling one way or another. It's up to you which one you choose.

06

A SETTLING BREATH

You can improve your play by taking a deep breath* during your pre-shot routine, just before walking toward the ball. As the breath flows out, imagine tension and anxiety flowing out with it. You'll naturally feel more grounded and settled, and find it easier to stay focused on your target and to swing with a more even tempo.

Breathe in mainly through your nose, feeling as if the air is pouring down the back of your throat, filling your whole torso from the bottom up, without letting your shoulders rise. Breathe out mainly through your lips, doing so a little more slowly than you breathed in. Hold your breath for a moment at the change of direction.

You may find it helpful to count as you inhale and exhale. For example, you could breathe in on a count of three: "In, two, three, and hold." And then breathe out on a slightly longer count: "Out, two, three, four, and hold." Use whatever numbers are comfortable for you.

You can also pair this exercise with a word that invites the feeling you are hoping to develop. For example, as you breathe in you could say, "Centered, two, three, and hold." As you breathe out you can say, "Settled, two, three, four, and hold." Words like "at ease," "calm," "grounded," or "softening" are also useful.

*Please note that if you have any respiratory difficulties you should not attempt any breathing techniques without consulting a health professional.

A. Ravielli

07

WHO'S IN CONTROL?

Have you ever hit a shot when it felt like you weren't really directing your swing, not trying to make it come out a particular way? The results are usually surprisingly good.

It may feel like you're not in control, but that's because you're used to trying to control your swing with your thinking mind. In fact, you haven't lost control—you've just transferred it to your subconscious mind. You've gotten out of your own way, which lets you play your best golf.

Here's a technique for intentionally turning over control to your subconscious mind. Before each swing, mentally say something to your body such as, "It's all yours," or "OK, take over." That acts as a signal for the thinking mind to let go, allowing the subconscious mind to guide the body in swinging the club without conscious interference. When you do that, the very best swing your body knows how to make will show up time after time.

To get the most out of your game, plan with your head but play from your heart.

08

YOUR PERSONAL PAR

There's a problem with par. Fewer than one in a hundred golfers has ever completed a round of golf in par or better, yet we all measure ourselves against it. We are disappointed when we don't hit a green in regulation (two less than par) and we often equate bogey with a less-than-successful effort. Trying to achieve par on a single hole is often a setup for failure for the average golfer, and a round at par is pretty much impossible.

Your day will be far more enjoyable if you set your own par for the course. Take your pencil and change the par written on the scorecard to reflect your handicap. If you have a nine handicap, add a stroke to par on the nine hardest holes. If it's a cold, windy day, give yourself another stroke or two. Now you have your "personal par" for the day. That's the appropriate standard by which to measure your performance.

Imagine how good it will feel to come in after the round and say, "I shot two under today!"

G. Ravielli

09

JUST COUNT THE GOOD ONES

They say that the best athletes have long memories of their successes and short memories of their failures. Once, when Jack Nicklaus was asked how to cure the shanks, he replied that he wouldn't know since he'd never hit one. Someone in the audience claimed to have seen him shank a shot, but Jack was adamant in his belief that it had never happened.

Your game will improve if you dwell more on the successes and pay less attention to the errors. Take the time to appreciate a good shot as it flies toward the target and settles down just where you planned. This will imprint a positive image in your mind and help to build your confidence.

After your round, skip the replays of what went wrong and what could have been. Instead, take the time to review the good decisions and the good shots you made. Do this often enough and the good ones will be all that you remember.

If you are a beginner or high-handicapper, you should use my special scoring system: just count the shots you liked. Give yourself a point for each, and make it your intention to get more points each time you play.

I've also taught this special system to better golfers, including tour pros, with much success. When they get too preoccupied with score, just counting the good ones shifts their attention to the quality of the shots they are playing. And when golfers of any level play more high-quality shots, their scores are bound to be lower.

10

GIVE YOURSELF A COMPLIMENT

Golfers need to do a better job of reinforcing the positive experience of a well-played shot. Too often when someone compliments one of our shots, we ascribe it to luck, replying with something like, "Even a blind squirrel finds an acorn once in a while."

Although you get points for humility, comparing yourself to a blind squirrel isn't going to build your confidence. You can make a different type of comment that will be more beneficial to your game.

When you hit a good shot that comes out just the way you wanted, go ahead and take credit for both the planning and execution. Reinforce your visualization skills by saying, "Thanks. That's just the way I pictured it." One of my favorite self-compliments for building confidence in both your ability and your routine is: "That's how I always hit it when I get out of my own way."

11

YOUR DOG WON'T BITE YOU

After his defeat in a playoff for the 1957 U.S. Open, Dr. Cary Middlecoff was asked how disappointed he was at losing his bid for a third Open title. He said, "It's not life and death. My wife will still love me and my dog won't bite me when I get home."

It's fine to take your golf seriously as long as you don't take *yourself* too seriously. It isn't much fun playing golf with people who get bent out of shape every time they hit a shot off line. Usually those people think they are better golfers than they actually are.

As one tour player said to his short-tempered amateur partner, "With all due respect, you're not really good enough to throw clubs."

Keep things in perspective and you'll enjoy yourself more on the golf course, and others will have more fun playing with you as well.

" The most important yardage on the golf course is the six inches between your ears."

Bobby Jones and Arnold Palmer

Mental G

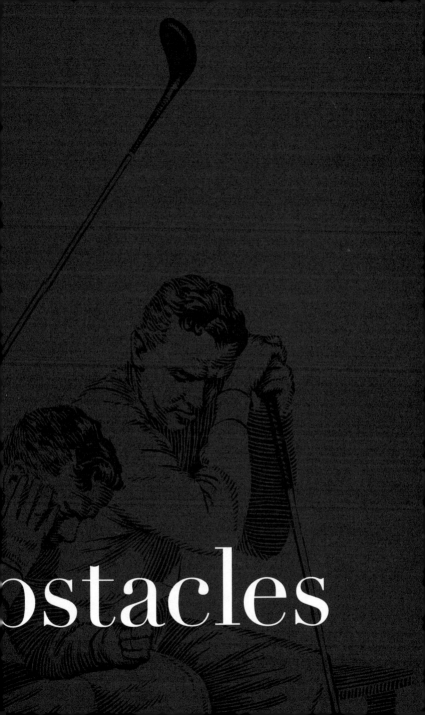

ostacles

12

RECOGNIZING AND UNDOING

You can work on your swing from dawn to dusk, but if you don't know how to work with your mind on the golf course, poor thinking, emotional reactions, and distractions will keep you from realizing your potential. You play your best golf when you are fully present and engaged, free from the interference of mental chatter, and free from the self-consciousness of over-analyzing your swing mechanics.

Improving your mental game involves two steps: The first step is *recognizing*. You need to cultivate awareness of what the real problem is. Usually it is not that something is missing. Rather, something is in the way. Once you discover the source of the interference, the second step is *undoing*.

The simplest way to change habits is to notice how often you are engaged in a habit and to make it your firm intention to do so less and less each day.

Change the self-defeating habit, whatever it may be, and nothing will be in the way of your best game showing up time after time.

13

GETTING BEYOND FEAR

The bigger deal we make of any shot, the more fear we have about a poor result. It can be the fear of embarrassment on the first tee in front of onlookers, the fear of failure in missing a short putt to win a hole, or the fear of ruining a good round with a poor drive on the last hole.

It doesn't do any good to deny the fact that we are experiencing fear. But we don't have to give in to fear: we can go beyond it.

To go beyond fear you first have to recognize and accept that you are feeling it. Put the fear in perspective by seeing that a golf shot is just one small event among the many that make up your life, and likely not among the top ten in importance.

After you put the shot into perspective, take a full breath to settle yourself, and release the tension that the fear produced. Replace the thoughts of bad results with positive images of the result you intend to bring about. Imagine the ball going in the hole or landing in the fairway, and commit to the shot you have planned. The best way to take your mind beyond the fear of what could go wrong is to get a feel for the swing you want to make and stay connected to a positive image of the target where you *do* want the ball to go.

A. Ravielli

14

WORKING WITH EMOTIONS

After a poor shot, most of us have an initial reaction of anger or frustration. Emotional reactions imprint more strongly in our memories than ordinary experiences. They get a special "tag" because of the energy associated with them. We're hard-wired that way. That's why it's best to get more excited about your good shots and less upset about your bad ones.

If you stockpile negative memories about a situation on the golf course (or elsewhere in your life), your confidence will be undermined. You'll be more likely to expect poor results in similar situations. And when you think that way, those expectations are likely to be fulfilled.

Not only do negative emotions imprint bad memories, they also limit your ability to learn from what just happened. Insight does not appear in the midst of emotional upheaval. Therefore, it's important to clear a negative emotional response to a shot as soon as possible. If you can keep your cool, you can reflect on what went wrong and adjust accordingly.

When you get upset, step aside, take a deep breath, and swing the club back and forth in an easy rhythm, focusing on the flowing feeling. The heat of emotion will subside more quickly that way, and it will be less likely to spoil the rest of your round.

15

PARALYSIS FROM ANALYSIS

A common malady in golf is called "paralysis from analysis." You're thinking about the twenty-three things you're supposed to remember to do, and the fourteen things you're supposed to remember *not* to do. After a while, you're not sure how to even hold the club, let alone swing it.

It's as if you're giving yourself a lesson during every swing. Thinking so much about mechanics gives you exactly that kind of swing—mechanical and awkward, the very opposite of a smooth, free-flowing motion.

There is an aspect of mind that engages in thinking, and a different aspect of mind that subconsciously operates the body.

Get your body and mind synchronized by turning your awareness toward feeling the flow and tempo of the swing. That allows your subconscious mind to run your body instead of your thinking mind directing your muscles to move this way and that. You'll make better swings, and you'll enjoy making them a lot more, too.

16

FIRST TEE JITTERS

If you're nervous on the first tee, perhaps you are concerned with what people will think of you if you hit a bad shot. Or perhaps you fear that starting your round with a bad shot means that the rest of the day will be a struggle.

Let me put your mind at ease. First, other players watching do not care that much about your tee shot. They are much more concerned about what will happen when *they* step up there. If any of the spectators are your friends, they certainly won't judge your game on the basis of one shot. The ones who don't know you probably won't either.

Second, you can probably remember many days when you didn't hit the first shot all that well, but after you got warmed up you played quite a good round.

Finally, put things in perspective. It's the first shot in a round of golf, not the beginning of the end of the world. Keep your sense of humor and enjoy your day.

17

DO YOU LISTEN TO YOUR THOUGHTS?

There's a difference between having a thought come to mind and acting on it. You can think about playing a risky shot, but you don't have to listen to that "bright idea." How many strokes would you save if you took a moment to reflect on the possible consequences of your decisions, rather than just doing the first thing that comes to mind?

After a good drive on a par five, for example, you may have the thought of playing a fairway wood to carry a water hazard fronting the green. You can either listen to that thought, or ask yourself, "Is the risk of a penalty stroke really worth the relatively small chance of getting on the green in two?" Take a moment and reflect on how confident you are in your ability to execute the shot. If you feel any doubt or find that you're talking yourself into going for it, it's probably a better idea to play a low-risk shot that takes the big number out of play. It will be easier to commit to that shot, be better for your score, and may even save you a golf ball.

18

MAKE SURE

Of all the things golfers may say to themselves as they prepare for a shot, in my opinion the two worst words are "make sure."

Make sure you don't hit your tee shot into the woods. *Make sure* you swing the club correctly. *Make sure* your pitch shot carries over that bunker. *Make sure* you don't leave that putt short. *Make sure* you don't run it too far by.

Giving yourself an instruction to make sure to do or not to do something immediately introduces self-consciousness and a try-hard mentality. That interferes with making a free, trusting swing or stroke, not to mention how exhausting it is to play shot after shot with the tension and pressure of making sure not to make a mistake! Trust in your process, and make the swing you practiced without burdening yourself with the baggage of *making sure*.

A. Ravielli

19

SELF-FULFILLING PROPHECY

Psychologically, fear produces the reaction of trying too hard to maintain control. If we're afraid of missing the fairway, we are overly cautious and hesitant. We try to steer the shot, make an awkward swing, and the ball heads for the rough. It's a self-fulfilling prophecy.

Physically, fear produces certain bodily reactions. Blood flows to our bigger muscles so we have less feel in our hands and make poor decisions with our brains. Adrenaline flows freely and we get speedy and jumpy.

The fear of a bad result can make our muscles tighten up during our swing. Afraid that we'll make a poor swing and get a bad result, we panic at the last instant. Sometimes this panic can manifest itself in an awkward, sudden movement, like the yips in putting. It's as if we're trying to swing and not to swing at the same time.

The remedy for this is to choose the shot that we feel most confident playing, pre-accept the range of possible results that might follow, and commit as fully as we can to our process without letting anxiousness over the outcome inhibit our abilities.

20

DON'T THINK OF A MONKEY

When we read, "Don't think of a monkey," a picture of a monkey instantly comes to mind. There isn't a specific image for the word "don't." That explains why we often follow the thought, "Don't chunk it into the bunker," with a chunk into the bunker.

Alternatively, the mind may take the word "don't" as a signal to create a negative action command. We'll try to produce whatever is most opposite of the image in the thought. For example, when you think, "Don't hit it out of bounds to the left," your mind may direct your body to send the ball as far from the left side as you can. That's why you find yourself in the woods on the right. You did a good job of not hitting it left, but not such a good job of getting it in the fairway.

Avoid the "don't" problem by always using a positive description of your intention. A single positive image is what you want your mind to give your body to execute. In the example above, "do" make your target the right side of the fairway. On the green, instead of saying, "Don't leave it short," *do* visualize your putt rolling firmly into the back of the cup.

21

YOU ARE SUCH A HACKER

Calling ourselves names is pretty common among golfers. The problem is that we not only say them, we hear them. And no matter how much we shrug it off as letting off steam, it gets in there and affects us.

If someone points and says, "That guy is a real hacker," we will expect him to hit a poor shot most every time. If you call yourself a hacker (or worse), you'll subconsciously expect to hit the next shot badly. That will make you worry about the bad result, and the tension in your swing will make that worry come true.

Instead, start changing the habit of calling yourself names. Put a mark on the bottom of your scorecard each time you say something bad about yourself. If you maintain the intention to change the habit, you'll see fewer and fewer marks on the card with each round. You'll probably start playing better, and you'll definitely feel better about yourself.

22

DON'T COMPLAIN ABOUT THE RAIN

Most people prefer the environment around them to be a particular way. Some people like to work where it's warm and there is background music playing; others like it cool and silent. Golfers are no different—we all have our favorite courses, playing conditions, and weather. When we don't get what we want, we start complaining.

There are several reasons we complain. First, we'd like someone to do something about it. Obviously, when it comes to the weather, complaining won't change things.

Also, we don't think it is fair if the course or the conditions don't favor our type of game. A long course with deep rough and lush fairways makes it tough for a short hitter. But who said golf is fair?

Finally, we complain to protect our egos. Our complaints give us an excuse in case we don't play well that day. "I would have done better if it hadn't been so windy."

Complaining only makes a bad situation worse. Accept the conditions and make the best of them. Practice in the rain and the wind, and you will have an advantage over other players in those conditions.

Instead of complaining, take Vijay Singh's attitude. When asked by a reporter if the rain that day would bother him, Vijay said, "Only if it's just raining on me."

23

KEEPING THINGS MOVING

Pace of play can be particu-
larly distracting to the type
of person who tends to take
responsibility for his or her whole foursome, as well
as for the group or groups behind them. When there's
a slow player in the foursome, the overly responsible
golfer often gets so preoccupied with the slow pace of
play that it starts getting in the way of his or her own
game. She starts hurrying her own routine, playing
faster to make up for the fact that the other person is
playing so slowly. This only makes things worse. She
ends up playing more shots, taking longer herself, and
feeling unhappy with the whole situation. Before she
realizes it, she's tied herself into knots.

If that happens to you, the best thing you can do is to address the situation before teeing off. Without singling anyone out, explain that it's crowded on the course today, and that you'd rather not hold people up and feel rushed to get out of their way. Ask if everyone in your foursome can agree to some ways to keep up a good pace of play.

By dealing with the issue from the start, you'll feel you've done everything you could to speed the pace of play. Keep up your end of the bargain by being ready to play when it is your turn. Do your best to let go of the feelings of responsibility for everyone else, and you'll have a better time on the golf course.

24 ME AND MY SHADOW

Players sometimes comment that their own shadow distracts them when they can see it during the swing. They peek to see how their swing looks, or it makes them self-conscious about how their swing looks to others.

If this is a problem for you, turn your attention toward bodily sensations during your setup and swing: feel your feet connecting with the ground, tune into good posture, and soften excess tension in your shoulders, arms, and hands. You will be less distracted by visual input like your shadow when you focus on feel.

On the other hand, your shadow can be helpful on the practice tee. With the sun at your back you can watch your shadow to check body positions as you swing back and through.

25

WAITING, WAITING, WAITING

When you find yourself waiting for the fairway or green in front of you to clear on every hole, it can feel like the round will never end. Sulking and complaining only make matters worse, for yourself and those who have to listen to you. It's easy for tempers to boil over. This is the time to keep your cool and find a way to make the best of a bad situation. Chat with your playing partners, do some stretching, or simply enjoy the scenery. Perhaps this will be the day you learn how to bounce the ball off the face of your wedge twenty times in a row.

Sometimes the situation is even worse: while you are waiting for the group in front you are getting hassled by the players behind you. What can you do? The first chance you have, go back to talk to them. You can usually make peace by saying, "We're waiting on every shot. We're sorry to hold you up. If you really want to play through, you're welcome to do so, but there isn't any place to go."

They'll say, "Thanks," and play through, or they'll say, "Never mind." Either way they'll be more understanding and stop pressing you. Communicating clearly about the situation is all you can do and often all you need to do.

26 GETTING AHEAD OF YOURSELF

We play our best golf when our minds are focused on the task at hand. That goes for anything we do. Getting ahead of yourself can land you in trouble.

Being fully present and engaged produces better results than being lost in daydreams. Worrying about a challenging hole you'll have to play later on or thinking about telling your friends at the bar about your great shots takes you out of the present and into the future. But if you're not focused on the shot you're facing now, you may not have a very good story to tell after the round.

When you find your mind has drifted into the future, take a moment to get reoriented to what's happening here and now. Make your plan, get a good picture of the shot, and swing away. There'll be time enough for daydreaming when the round is done.

27

ON GETTING ADVICE

Golfers are generally well meaning and often try to help others. These good intentions sometimes show up on the course in the form of freely offered advice. Unfortunately, in most cases the advisor is not a golf teacher but a fellow weekend golfer who has heard a tip on television or read it in a magazine and is anxious to share. Even when they're accurate, such tips often focus on swing mechanics, get you thinking about how you swing, and cause more problems than they solve.

So what do you do when you are playing with a self-appointed instructor? The safest thing to do is to thank them for their interest and express appreciation for the valuable information they are sharing with you. Then forget about it and focus on your process the best you can. If they press more unrequested advice on you, explain that the pro you take lessons from wants you to work on your game in a particular way and not talk to people about it.

In general, be polite but find a way to play your own game.

28

FIND SOMETHING GOOD ABOUT IT

Most golfers are expert critics. We can all find something wrong with even the very best shot. If it doesn't go in the hole, either it was too short or too long, too far left or too far right. We can even criticize a putt that *does* go in for rolling too fast or too slow as it gets to the cup.

If the first thing we say about a shot is what went wrong, eventually we'll feel like we have to go back to the drawing board and relearn how to swing.

Try changing that habit by making the intention to say something good about any shot that is at all usable. Chances are you did more things right than wrong, and a slight adjustment will make the next shot a really good one.

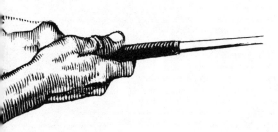

> "The more I practice,
> the luckier I get."
>
> *Ben Hogan, Gary Player, Arnold Palmer*
> *Tom Watson, and Lee Trevino*

Practice
Preparat

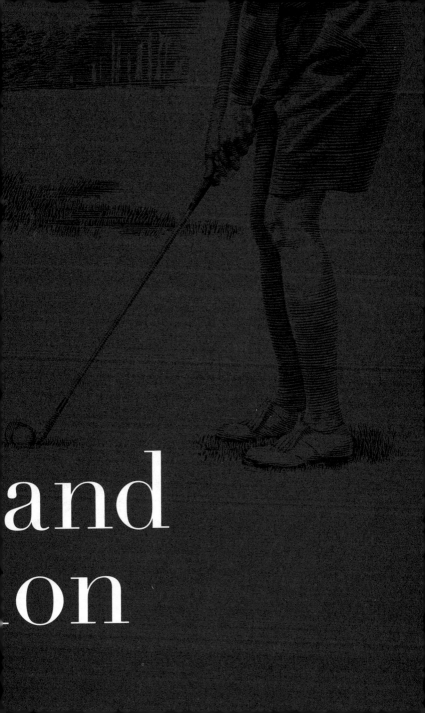

and
on

29

PRACTICE WITH PATIENCE

Golfers are always looking for the secret, that one tip that will make their swing come together that very moment and let them play golf happily ever after.

Sadly, not even Ben Hogan's secret worked that way. A fix-it tip is like a patch on a coat. Just as patches eventually fall off, quick fixes don't last. A champion's skills don't come easily; they require the patient mastery of golf's fundamentals. There's no substitute for working hard to groove a good technique until it becomes second nature. As I wrote in *Zen Golf*, "Train it until you trust it, and trust it before you try it."

Hogan kept notes of what he was working on and what he accomplished in each session. Practice with a plan, and with patience, knowing that your hard work will bear fruit in the future.

30

TRAIN FOR COMPETITION

Use at least part of your practice time to toughen yourself for competition. Have putting contests on the practice green, with friends or as self-competitions against a target score. Practice in the short-game area until you get up and down a certain number of times. Hit shots out of a bunker until you get a certain number within six feet of the hole.

Gary Player took his self-competition and the added pressure very seriously. He was once late for a dinner party he was hosting at his own home because he had set the requirement for himself that he wasn't going to leave the practice green until he'd made twenty putts in a row from five feet away.

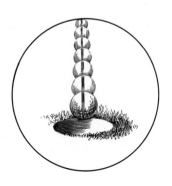

31

THE SENDING RANGE

Golfers sometimes get so concerned with hitting the ball that they forget that the purpose of the swing is to send the ball toward their target. That's why you see some players with practice swings that look pretty good, passing through the bottom of the swing arc, sweeping along the grass in the direction of the target.

Then they step up to the ball and chop down on it as if they were using an axe to split a log. They are swinging as if the *ball* were their target.

It's a problem if you think that your job is to hit *at* the ball, because you won't put enough energy into following through properly *past* the ball. But if you think that your job is to *send* the ball toward the target, you'll make a much better swing toward and past the impact zone and into your follow-through.

I was very proud of two young students who once left a note on my desk saying, "Doc, we're out on the sending range, sending balls to targets."

32

SHOW YOUR TRUE SWING

When you go for a lesson from a swing instructor and he or she asks you to hit a few shots, don't make what you think is a pretty-looking swing or try to make the ball go straight. It's common to try to produce a good shot for your instructor, but that often masks the swing habits you have developed. It is much more important to swing without self-consciousness, releasing any extra tension generated because you're being watched. Take the attitude of swinging without interference from a concern for results, either about how the swing looks or where the ball goes, and make your most ordinary swing. (I've suggested to a number of teaching pros that they tell their students to hit a few shots to warm up while they tend to something else, then watch without the students knowing it.)

If all you are showing your instructor is how you think your swing should look, he or she will be coaching you based on what you demonstrate, rather than addressing your actual habits.

33

HOW TO GROOVE A SWING CHANGE

When you get a lesson that changes the way you swing a club, you need to train your body to make that new move. You want it to feel natural and you don't want to have to think about it. This takes some time and some work. Here's the fastest way to groove your swing.

Start by moving your body without a club. Take your stance with arms crossed and hands on shoulders (for work on your legs or torso), or arms extended with palms facing each other. Then move through the swing path and hold your finish position. Do this fifteen to twenty times.

Next, make the same number of repetitions swinging a club, but without hitting a ball.

Then make fifteen to twenty swings hitting a ball but without a target—or concern for where the ball goes. Your only objective is to swing the same way as you did when there was no ball.

Finally, use your full routine to play shots with a variety of clubs to different targets, each time assessing how well you produced the move you are learning.

Carry out this sequence several times and you'll have made a good start toward grooving that new way of swinging.

A. Ravielli

34

A SOLID CORE

In the martial arts and similar mind-body traditions of the East, the body's "center of gravity" is the source from which all movement and energy flow. It is located a few inches below the navel, in the center of the torso. This center of gravity is the focal point for much of the golf swing.

During your pre-shot routine, as you release your breath fully, feel your weight settle down in or below your center of gravity. In the backswing, when you make a good turn away from the target, it is your center of gravity that you coil around. As you make the transition and uncoil, your core muscles are the source from which all the power of your swing emanates. And when you make a good finish, it is your center of gravity that is pointing directly at the target.

Physical training to strengthen the core muscles that surround your center of gravity will help you establish the foundation of a powerful golf swing.

35

BETTER PUTTING FOR BETTER DRIVING

If you're not confident on your short putts, you'll feel pressure to lag your long putts quite close to the hole to avoid three-putting. You know that the best way to have easier first putts is to play the shortest iron possible for your approach shots. To get into short-iron range, you'll press to hit your drives as far as you can. That can lead to a lot of poor tee shots.

However, if you feel more at ease with short putts, you won't worry so much about your shots into the green. And if you don't worry about your approach shots, you won't put pressure on yourself to hit your tee shots as far as possible. That will let you trust your routine and make more ordinary, unforced swings.

Spend time practicing short putts and you'll improve the rest of your game, too.

36

PRACTICE PUTTING WITHOUT A HOLE

Isolating the components of putting in order to sharpen them one at a time is an ideal way to practice. The first thing to work on is the stroke, and the best way to practice the stroke is without a hole.

Get comfortable in your setup, aimed toward an area of the green where there is no hole. Make an ordinary stroke, not too big or small—whatever your intuition creates without conscious intention. Keep your head and body as steady as you can. Focus on the tempo of the putterhead swinging back and through, and the feel of the putterface at impact.

Keep putting without a hole until you feel your stroke to be one of ease and flow, you feel consistent, solid sweet-spot contact, and you see the ball rolling smoothly, end over end.

The nice thing about this practice is that—since there's no hole—you can't miss.

37

WARMING UP

First things first: Stretch and make baseball-style swings to loosen up so that you don't hurt yourself when you start hitting balls.

Start your warm-up by making half-swings with a wedge or nine-iron. Focus on good tempo and crisp contact through the impact zone. Follow those with some three-quarter swings, then go to full swings, maintaining the same tempo and focus on good contact throughout. Work your way through your clubs from short to long.

Know the difference between a *warm-up* session before a round and a *practice* session. Try to avoid working on your swing technique in a warm-up session, and instead save that for a practice session after the round or on another day.

38

TAKING YOUR RANGE GAME TO THE COURSE

Many of my lessons start with the player claiming to be a far lower "handicap" on the range than on the course. That's why it's said that the longest walk on a golf course is from the practice range to the first tee. One of the reasons for this is the way many players warm up. Beating a dozen balls on the range with one club, then doing it again with another, and so on, may be good for working up a sweat, but it won't get you into the rhythm of actually playing golf. On the course, you play one shot with a driver, the next with a seven-iron, and so on.

Here's a way you can get into your course rhythm before you tee off: Near the end of your warm-up session, think of three holes—a par three, par four, and par five —that you know well. Pretend that you are playing those holes, using the clubs you normally would.

When you get to the first tee, you'll feel like you've already played a few holes and will be in your on-course rhythm.

39

THE SWING KEY

People ask what the best swing thoughts are, but it seems to me that it's better to feel the way you want to swing rather than think about swing mechanics. That's why I prefer to call them swing keys: feelings or images that the body is already familiar with and capable of executing. In general, it's helpful if such swing keys include the tempo or the feel you desire as you move through the impact zone.

The ideal swing key clusters several elements of the swing into a familiar movement or sensation. This is much more effective than an instruction to yourself on how to make the swing happen.

A swing key such as "long arms through impact" is a good example. It counteracts the tendency to pull in your arms near contact, causing you to hit thin or topped shots. The long-arms image simply conveys what you want your swing to feel like, rather than instructional techniques about how to move your arms, like telling yourself to extend your arms downward and outward near impact. Directing your muscles that way doesn't work very well. Feeling-based swing keys help you swing with more trust, more flow, and more consistency.

A. Ravielli

40

HAND IT OVER

"Holding a tray" is a classic swing key that's taught to give a feel for the proper position of the right hand (for right-handed golfers) at the top of the backswing. The idea is to have the wrist fully hinged and the palm facing skyward, supporting the shaft of the club. Instructors often tell a player to feel like he or she is balancing a tray full of drinks in their right hand, above their shoulder, at that point in the swing.

However, not many golfers have waited tables, let alone carried a tray of drinks over their shoulders. The point of a swing key is to use a movement the person already knows how to make without having to think about it.

I told a poker player (who'd never carried a tray in his life) to imagine that he is sitting at a card table when someone whom he doesn't like but who owes him some money walks in behind him. I told him to reach up and back over his shoulder with his hand out and say, "Hand over the money." He used that as his swing key for his next shot and hit the best seven-iron of his life.

41

SKIPPING A ROCK

Another classic swing key is "skipping a rock." Many of us recall finding a small, flat stone and throwing it low and from the side to make it skip as many times as possible across a calm lake or pond.

The action that makes the stone skim the surface comprises several movements that many swing coaches regard as important elements of a good golf swing. These movements include your weight shifting forward,

your hips turning, your upper body staying back a bit, your right elbow (for right-handers) passing close to the body, and your right wrist staying cocked until just before release.

Instead of training each movement individually, this swing key lets you access a cluster of movements, with natural sequence and timing, with which your body is already quite familiar. That lets you incorporate them into your golf swing in less time and with less of the self-conscious, mechanical thinking that will interfere with a flowing swing.

42

GET TO THE FINISH

Working backward from your goal is often helpful. Here's a swing key that uses this approach.

Make a practice swing with a mid-iron into what you and your instructor agree is a good finish position. Hold that finish for a few seconds, with as much awareness of how your body feels as possible, thinking, "This is the finish I want to get to at the end of my swing." Do this several times to ingrain the feeling.

When you play, make a practice swing before each shot, holding a good finish position for a second or two. Your swing key is, "Finish like that."

The benefit of this key is that your subconscious mind senses your body positions throughout the swing, and will do its best not to let your body make a backswing or a transition at the top from which you won't be able to finish in the position you intend. Your body will find it difficult to make a bad swing and get to a good finish.

"Ask yourself how many shots you would have saved if you always developed a strategy before you hit, always played within your capabilities, never lost your temper, and never got down on yourself."

Jack Nicklaus

100 YDS

Course S

rategy

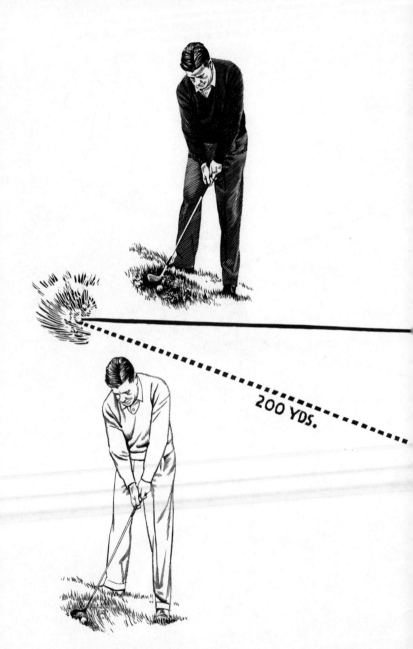

200 YDS.

43

COURSE MANAGEMENT

Follow Tommy Armour's two-part formula for course management:

First, play the shot you're most comfortable playing. Second, aim toward the place that gives you your easiest next shot.

It's that simple. It takes discipline and thinking outside the box to hit an iron off the tee on a par five or to aim away from the hole with an approach shot.

However, if you follow T.A.'s recipe, you'll enjoy some deliciously low scores.

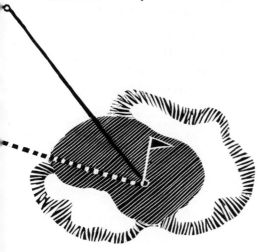

44

THINKING OUTSIDE THE BOX

Today's a good day to start thinking outside the box. We limit ourselves with our assumptions and superstitions. Is there a rule that says you have to use a driver on every par four or par five, or that you have to go for every green in regulation? Looking at things with a different perspective increases your choices dramatically and allows for far more creativity.

Tom Watson, one of the best golfers of his time, said, "It takes courage to lay up on a par three. But it may be the smartest play for the situation." Billy Casper won the 1959 U.S. Open at Winged Foot Golf Club, and part of the credit is due to his ability to think outside the box on a tough par three. At the 220-yard third hole, Casper—to the bewilderment of his fellow competitors—laid up in front of the green all four rounds. He made par every time.

45

THE PLAY CLUB

In the nineteenth century, the club with which you teed off wasn't called a driver—it was called your "play club." That difference in language can be helpful for your game. When we hear "driver," we think of something like a pile driver pounding logs into the earth, making massive, powerful blows. We swing the driver like we're trying to knock the cover off the ball.

They called it the play club because of its function—to put the ball into play. There is no reference to how far or how hard you can hit it. It also doesn't have to be the biggest club you own, nor even the same club on every hole. It's the club you choose to use to put the ball into play. Think about how much better you'd score if you thought about the club you use off the tee as your play club.

46

HOW FAR WERE YOU TRYING TO HIT IT?

Most golfers swing their drivers as hard as they can. It adds a new game, one based on ego: "Whose tee shot goes the farthest?"

There's a fascination with the power game and how long we can hit it off the tee. New technology creates more and more powerful clubs. If you've got last year's model, you might get a case of driver envy.

How far you hit a tee shot is good for a long-drive contest, but it is not the measure of your golf game. If you want lower scores, accuracy and consistency are much more important.

The pros know how important it is to play within themselves, swinging at about 80 percent on most shots. That produces a smoother, more consistent swing, and enables them to control direction better and hit the ball more solidly. Off-center impact costs you more yardage than a slightly slower swing speed.

On the tee, pick a distance down the fairway you feel you can reach without swinging out of your shoes. That will let you make a smoother swing, which will give you a better chance for solid contact on the clubface. You'll hit more fairways, and probably find that each drive goes farther than you expected.

47

BE YOUR OWN CADDIE

If you were caddying for a good friend in a tournament, you wouldn't scold him when he hit a bad shot, nor would you suggest that he play a low-percentage shot that could cost him a lot of strokes. You'd probably be positive and supportive, encourage him to think through his plans for every shot, and be sure he was settled and ready before he played each shot.

Why not be a good caddie for yourself? Keep your self-talk positive, remind yourself of the key points of your routine, and choose the shot you'd recommend to a player of your ability if you were caddying for him.

48

MATCH PLAY STRATEGY

Bobby Jones said that his career as a champion began when he "stopped playing against the other fellow and started playing against Old Man Par."

It's important to keep your focus as much as possible on your own game, even in match play. That way your opponent's performance won't influence you so much. Your ultimate measure of success is how well you play the golf course. You're not competing directly against the other golfer; you both play the same hole and compare how well you each did. The one who did better against the course wins the hole.

Make your goal to play each hole the best you can, without letting the other player's game take you out of yours.

49

I HIT THIS CLUB THAT FAR ONCE

Average golfers almost always leave their approach shots far short of the hole. Ego is at fault: we choose the club that would reach the hole only if we hit it absolutely perfectly. A perfect shot is quite unlikely, which is why we very rarely reach our targets. Instead, when faced with an approach to a green, choose the club that will take you to the back of the green with a perfect shot. More often than not, you'll end up in the middle.

Golfers also commonly suffer from delusions of grandeur. When asked how far they hit a particular iron, many golfers' answers are based on the longest shot they ever hit with that club. When I asked one golfer why he had chosen a seven-iron for an uphill, into-the-wind shot of 170 yards, he replied, "I hit this club that far once." No matter that there was a strong helping wind, that it was steeply downhill, or that it landed on a firm green and rolled an extra ten yards. No wonder he left almost all of his approach shots short of the green.

An amateur once asked Sam Snead how he puts backspin on long iron shots. Snead asked how often the player hit his shots past the pin. When the golfer said that he rarely did, Sam asked, "Then why in heck would you want them to spin backward?"

50

OVERCOMPENSATION

One of the obstacles to playing a good shot is the memory of one that was not so good. Instead of simply playing the shot we are facing, we are more interested in avoiding a repeat of the poor shot we hit last time.

If you leave a twenty-foot putt three feet short, the next time you have a similar putt you think, "Don't leave it short." You haven't given yourself an image of the putt you *did* want to hit; the only plan is, "Anything but short." And the surest way not to leave it short is to hit the ball six feet past the hole. Good job of not leaving it short!

To prevent this pattern of overcompensation, don't leave the scene of a poor shot or poor club selection without this post-shot routine: Reflect on the cause and make another swing that applies the correct decision or proper swing key that would have worked better. That allows you to leave memories of the bad shot behind and take the feel of the correct shot with you. The next time you face a similar situation you'll have a positive plan and are likely to play a better shot.

51

DON'T PLAY PREVENT DEFENSE

The great champion Bobby Jones considered his most serious weakness to be his tendency to play in an overly cautious style in order to avoid mistakes. He found that when he was comfortably ahead in a tournament, he began to fear the embarrassment of not holding his lead. He would try to control his swing to avoid making a mistake. Instead of picking a positive target, he focused on staying out of hazards. He said that he would have won many more tournaments early in his career had he focused on his targets as much when leading as when chasing.

What did Bobby do about it? Instead of playing a sort of "prevent defense," he stayed with his game plan, taking note of the hazards but plotting a strategy of positive targets: places on the fairway that would give him a wide berth from the hazard but still leave good angles of approach to the green, and places on the green that were far enough from greenside hazards but would still leave him with reasonable putts. That formula produced the Grand Slam, the best year of golf anyone had ever played.

G. Ravielli

52

RIGHT SIDE OR LEFT SIDE?

There is a commonly taught formula to determine the ideal place to tee the ball between the tee-markers. If your usual shot shape (or the one you intend to play on that hole) is a fade, set up toward the right side of the tee box. If you're playing a draw, tee the ball more toward the left.

Instead of simply following the formula, use your intuition to get as comfortable for your tee shots as you can. Walk slowly from one of the tee-markers to the other, looking out toward your landing area as you walk. Be aware of the degree to which you feel more or less at ease with the view at each step. When your eyes and your instincts match up, you've found the spot to tee it up that's going to be most comfortable for you to make a confident and committed swing.

53

THE DREADED STRAIGHT BALL

Many golfers planning to play a fade or a draw aim toward the rough on the side of the fairway they expect their ball to curve away from. That gives them the most fairway possible, in case the gentle fade they hoped for turns into a wicked slice.

But what happens if they happen to hit the rare one that flies straight and true, directly where they aimed? How sad that such a good shot ends up in the rough!

There are those who choose to aim down the middle and try to hit it straight—but then if they fade or draw the ball a little too much, it goes off the

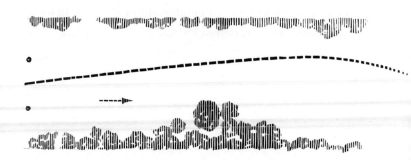

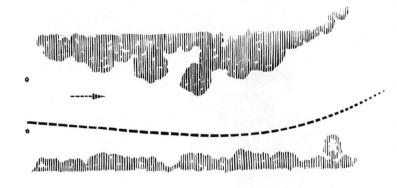

fairway. It seems like it's just a matter of choosing the lesser of two evils.

Here's an alternative that will give you the best of both worlds. Starting from the edge of the rough on the side you intend the ball to turn away from, move your eyes one third of the way across the fairway. Make that your aiming point. If the ball curves as expected, you have two-thirds of the fairway to work with. And if you do hit the ball straight, you'll still finish on the fairway. There are even a few yards of extra room to receive a little push or pull in the unexpected direction.

You will feel more confident, and will trust yourself to make a freer swing, knowing that you've allowed yourself the most leeway on the fairway for whichever way the ball bounces.

54

RIGHT THERE IN FRONT OF YOU

An intermediate target is what some golfers use to help ensure that they have good alignment at address. They find something distinctive a few feet in front of the ball, in line with the target they're aiming at in the distance.

On the fairway, you have to use whatever you find there, such as a small leaf or little patch of clover. However, on the tee box you get to choose where you place your tee, anywhere between the tee-markers. Once you've chosen the part of the tee box from which you want to play, find an old divot, a discolored bit of turf, or even a broken tee that was left on the ground, and tee up your ball straight behind it on the line toward your chosen target. It's up to you where you tee it up, so why not take advantage of the alignment aids that are right there in front of you?

55

GET OVER IT

Getting upset over a bad shot is understandable. And a few seconds of emotion isn't really a problem. The problem comes from carrying it with you in a way that negatively affects the next shot and leads to a downward spiral of poor play.

It's okay to get mad, but then get over it. Tiger Woods has a ten-yard rule. He allows himself to be mad about a shot, but only until he has walked ten yards toward the next shot. From then on, he has let go of the last shot and is focused only on the one in front of him.

Here's how to be like Tiger and get over a bad shot: After the intensity of your initial reaction passes, take a deep breath or two. Feel the negativity flow out as you exhale, and channel the energy into a positive process. Make one or two practice swings until you make the one you would have rather made on the previous shot. The difference you feel tells you what you need to do to best prepare for your next shot.

This post-shot routine gives you two benefits as you walk away from a bad shot. Your last swing is a good one rather than a bad one, and your focus turns away from negative emotions and toward a positive feeling for what you need to do to make the next shot a good one.

56

HOW TO BREAK 100

Breaking 100 is about playing within yourself. Acknowledge that you are not playing at the level of a single-digit handicapper. You can break 100 without making a scorecard par on a single hole. Nine bogeys and nine double bogeys equal 99 (or 97 on a par-70 course).

Lower your expectations for each shot to realistically match the range of results you usually experience so you don't get too frustrated. Don't try to play tricky shots that give you little chance of a good result and can lead to a blow-up hole. Allow for your "personal par," an extra stroke or two on every hole. Instead of par on a given hole being three, four, or five, for you it will be four, five, or six—and maybe even seven on a very long hole!

It's better not to keep a running total of your score. Most golfers at your level get nervous when they have to shoot a certain score on the last few holes to break 100.

Finally, make your target score a 95. That way, even if you miss by a shot or two, you'll still break 100!

57

HOW TO BREAK 90

Breaking 90 is not about making more birdies, or even pars. It's about making fewer big numbers.

Check your course management decisions. Don't attempt so many risky low-percentage shots. They may be spectacular when they come off the way you planned, but they usually don't—and when they don't, you're looking at a big number.

Take your medicine and pitch out to the fairway when you drive it into the deep rough. Lay up instead of trying to hit a hero shot over a lake with your three-wood.

If you make mostly bogeys and the pars outnumber the double bogeys, you'll break 90!

58

HOW TO BREAK 80

Breaking 80 is about saving par. To break 80 on a par-72 golf course, you have to make more pars than bogeys.

Assuming you already manage your game well enough to avoid playing too many risky shots and making big numbers, you'll need to work on increasing the number of times you get up and down when you miss the green. You will also need to work on reducing the number of three-putts when you are on the green but far from the hole.

Work on your short game to get up and down more often. Arrange your practice schedule so that you spend more time on shots within sixty yards of the hole than on full swing shots on the range. On the practice green, roll a lot of thirty- and forty-foot putts. Feel for pace is the most important factor in avoiding three-putts.

If you make two pars for every bogey, and enough birdies to offset any double bogeys, you'll break 80!

"I never hit a shot without having a clear picture of it in my mind. I see where I want the ball to finish. I see the path, trajectory, and how it will land. I see the kind of swing that will produce that shot. Only then do I address the ball."

Jack Nicklaus

Golfing Ball

Your

59 VISUALIZATION

In preparing for a golf shot, create as vivid and complete an image as possible—all the sights, sounds, and feels you can imagine will happen when you swing the club, make impact, and send the ball on its path to the target.

Your subconscious mind runs your body through images. When you eat, you have an image of tasting that delicious bite of food, and your body knows how to deliver it to your mouth without thinking about it. When you use your imagination that way, your body gets clear instructions as to where you'd like the ball to go, and your thoughts don't interfere with how you're going to get it there.

When you play golf, do your best to have a clear, vivid, and precise image of where you want the ball to go, and trust your body to do its best to send it there.

60

COMMITMENT

Commitment means playing a shot without doubt about whether or not it's the right shot to play, and without fear about how it will turn out.

What if a hard seven-iron was actually a smarter choice than a soft six? Committing to the swing you prepared for with the seven-iron will give you a better result than swinging the six-iron with doubt in your mind. As U.S. Open champion Tom Kite said, "In planning a golf shot, the only correct choice is the decisive one."

Establish a strong intention to maintain your commitment. Rate yourself on each shot for how well you stayed committed to your plan for that swing, from takeaway to follow-through. Make it your goal to keep improving your level of commitment from round to round, and you'll see your scores get lower and lower.

61

PROGRAM A GOOD SWING

There may be a particular move that you trust to anchor your swing. You'll have the best chance of executing that move if you focus on it *before* you play the shot, rather than thinking about it *while* you are swinging.

Stand well behind the ball and make two or three partial swings. The most important thing is to produce the feeling of the specific move you want to make. This "programs" your body to do its best to make a good swing.

Rather than making a full swing at full speed, it's more effective to program your move using a partial swing, one that lets you get a good feel for the way your body and your club are moving. Use whatever works best for you to get that feel. After swinging that way a couple of times, tell yourself that the move is programmed in. Like a computer, you program it and let it run.

After making your programming swings, picture the shot you're playing, take a full breath, and let it all the way out. Walk forward without rushing and address the ball. There is no longer any need to think about how you're going to make your swing. Trust that you've done your best to program your move, and swing away.

62

TEMPO, TEMPO, TEMPO

Perhaps the most important aspect of breathing in the pre-shot routine is breathing out fully before approaching the ball. When you do, you have a better chance of swinging smoothly. That's because your tempo at the start of your approach sets the tempo for your swing. When you rush to the ball, you're more likely to make a quick, hurried swing. Completing the breath is an ideal way to settle yourself so you can begin your approach with the tempo you want for your swing.

When you set up to the ball you need to maintain that same tempo. There can be a tendency to rush into the swing to get it over with. You need to be firmly set, free of distracting thoughts, and ready to swing from your center of gravity. Just as you should finish the breath before starting your approach, finish the set-up before starting your swing. On the other hand, remember that you can disrupt your tempo if you spend too long hovering over the ball.

Maintain your tempo throughout your pre-shot routine and into your backswing. The most common problem in swing tempo happens at the transition to your downswing. Finish taking the club back and gather your energy with a feeling of a slight pause before starting the club down and forward. Take your time in the transition and you'll make a better move through the ball.

63

REMOVING TENSION

An important part of preparing for a golf shot is clearing excess muscle tension, because tension is an obstacle to flow. There needs to be just enough tension to provide good posture and to maintain control of the club during the swing. Any more than that interferes with making a fluid, powerful golf swing.

To remove excess tension, rest your awarenes on the area of your body where you're feeling the tension and imagine that, like a snowflake in the morning sun, the tension melts in the light of awareness. If the tension seems to persist stubbornly in a particular place in the body, imagine that each breath you take flows in and out of that area, as if the breath were dissolving the tension in those muscles as it moves through them.

Tension and deep breathing are incompatible. If you're tense, you won't be breathing deeply; if you breathe deeply, tension dissolves. By incorporating a full breath into your swing routine for every shot, you will find an ideal "trigger" for the start of your approach to the ball.

64

YOUR FAVORITE TEE SHOT

Every now and again you will come across a tee shot that just doesn't suit your eye. There may even be one on your home course. You find it hard to get comfortable no matter where you tee the ball between the markers. In that situation, it's not easy to commit to a target for aiming. The lack of commitment makes it hard to swing freely, and your results will be inconsistent. That only increases your discomfort on the tee the next time.

To get more comfortable, imagine that you're standing on your favorite tee box, one on which you almost always feel confident about hitting a good drive. Standing behind the ball, pick a place in the fairway you'd like the ball to land, and aim in a way that accounts for the shape of your usual ball flight when you play from your favorite tee box. After you set your club at address and take your stance, don't look toward the fairway again. Just imagine that what's out there is the fairway that receives your favorite tee shot, and swing away as if you were really playing that hole.

This technique will let you make a swing that's more free and confident, and you'll have a much better chance of a good outcome wherever you're playing.

65

GOLF PHYSICS

Many high handicappers don't understand the physics of club design. They think they have to help the ball get up in the air by swinging upward at the ball. Unfortunately, for an approach shot from the fairway, if you swing up into the ball only two things can happen, and both are bad.

Since the ball is sitting on the ground, to swing upward into it you have to be coming from beneath it, meaning that the clubhead will hit the ground first, resulting in a fat shot. If you miss the ground as you swing upward into the ball, the leading edge of the clubface will hit the upper half of the ball, resulting in a topped or thin shot. Solid contact comes only from trusting that the club will do its job if you do yours: swinging crisply downward through impact.

66

REHEARSE YOUR SHORT GAME SWING

Here's how to blend intuition and technique to produce good chips and pitches, and to improve your game as you play.

First, in a place a few feet away from the ball, find some grass similar to your lie. Take a couple of swings through that grass to get a feel for how it will affect the club and how firmly you'll need to swing the clubhead through it.

Knowing the quality of the grass through which you'll be swinging, plan the type of shot you'll play. Picture how the ball will fly, how it will release, and how it will roll out toward the hole.

Then take your stance nearer to the ball, making rehearsal-type practice swings until you feel that the size and force of the swing you just made will be most likely to produce the shot you pictured.

Finally, step into your actual stance and do your best to reproduce the feel and size of that swing.

When you reproduce the swing you intended, you'll either get the result you pictured or learn that you needed to make a bigger, smaller, firmer, or softer swing. That way you will learn from every shot and get better and better at judging the swings you need to make to get the results you're looking for from your chips and pitches.

67

GET ON THE SAME PAGE

Have you ever seen a player make a lot of practice swings with one club, then change his or her mind and switch clubs just before addressing the ball? Often the result is less than what was hoped for.

The problem is that your mind can change quickly, but the feel for a movement ingrained in the body through practice swings takes longer to replace with a new feel. When you change your mind about how you're going to play a shot just before you execute it, you need to give your body time to tune in to the same plan as your mind. That tuning in can take up to ten seconds. You need to give yourself that much time if you are changing to a shorter or longer club when the wind shifts, or changing your mind from playing a draw to playing a fade, and so on.

If you make a new plan or switch clubs, take plenty of rehearsal swings with the new image in mind, and get used to the new feel. Then you can flow through your routine with your body and mind on the same page.

68

NO MORE ANYWAYS

When you know that something is wrong with your preparation for the shot you're about to play, it's a common mistake to override your intuition and go ahead anyway. That's why I call those shots "anyways."

You might have the feeling that the ball is too far from you. You might have the nagging thought that you don't have enough club, or the feeling that something's not quite right. But you think, "I'll just go ahead and hit it anyway."

Your body knows when your mind is uncomfortable and will compensate the best it can. Sometimes you swing a little harder, steer the ball to the right or left, or start to think about technique as you start your swing. The result is rarely good.

Think of how many strokes you could save by stopping to adjust your stance or re-tee the ball—instead of just going ahead anyway. Start your routine over with a deep breath, and return to focusing on making a free, confident swing.

69

STEP OUT OF THE BATTER'S BOX

Before making a swing, you might find yourself standing over the ball, trying to get comfortable, checking your alignment, or reviewing a list of techniques for the swing you're about to make. If you get stuck at address, standing there longer than usual, you'll have trouble making a swing with good tempo.

Take a tip from major league baseball. The batter waggles the bat and is constantly moving as he waits for the pitch. If the pitcher takes too long, the hitter may start to feel stale. So he will step out of the batter's box, taking a time out. Then he'll step back into the box, take his stance, waggle the bat, and be ready for the pitch.

If you feel like you've been over the ball too long and your routine has lost its flow, take a step back with your front foot. Take a breath, let it out, and step back in. Settle, waggle, and swing away.

If you can't get comfortable, go back behind the ball, do a quick review of your plan for the shot and start your routine from the beginning. It may take a few seconds more, but it will take less time than looking in the woods for your ball.

70

TOO GOOD A SHOT

Golfers sometimes get upset when they hit a shot better than they expected. A drive is hit so solidly that it runs through the fairway into the rough, or an iron shot is struck so purely that it flies the green. Yes, you got a bad break, but only because you hit the shot especially well. Fixating on the negative outcome robs you of the positive part of the experience. You miss the joy of executing a great shot, and end up feeling bad instead of good about it. To reinforce your confidence, focus on the quality of the shot more than on where it finished.

Also, getting upset about a shot can interfere with your ability to play your next one. Feeling bad about the result of a good shot sends a negative message to your body. It's like saying, "Let's not hit one that well in the future." Wouldn't it be better to feel good about the process (regardless of the result), and send a message to your body that you'd like more where that came from?

If you keep hitting shots through the fairway or over the green, that's good, not bad. It's a sign you're getting longer. Now you can cut the corner on those doglegs and use shorter irons for your approaches.

Congratulations!

71

BAILING OUT

You see trouble on the left, and hit the shot miles to the right. What happened? The key to understanding why we involuntarily bail out is a simple principle: your intentions shape your actions. Your primary intention is to stay away from the trouble on the left. You have in mind where you don't want to go, but no positive direction of where you do want the shot to finish. The result is a good job of avoiding one side, but not such a good job of hitting the fairway.

A better approach is to take the hazard into account when choosing where to aim. To make a free swing without bailing out you need to pre-accept that you can handle wherever the shot goes, that there's nothing you're trying to avoid. Choose a shot that gives you a usable result with minimum risk. Once you have a positive target in the fairway or on the green, make it your intention to send the ball there.

A. Ravielli

72

CHANGE YOUR MIND, NOT YOUR SWING

Even the best golfers hit real stinkers once in a while. If one of those shows up, take a deep breath to get over the frustration. Then comment on it in a detached way, saying something like, "Hmm, interesting. How unlike me. What got in the way?"

After a really bad shot, the most common tendency is to review your swing mechanics, as if you forgot how to swing from one shot to the next. That is highly unlikely. It usually has more to do with your state of mind than the state of your swing.

Think about how you prepared for your shot, how committed you were to playing the shot you planned. There's probably less need to fix your swing technique than there is to prepare better before you swing.

If you felt good about your preparation, commitment, and tempo, check your alignment. It's possible you actually made a very good swing and that the only reason it ended up in the woods is that you aimed there. Correcting your aim may be all you need to do.

If you see an unwanted pattern showing up shot after shot, simply adjust your setup, tune in to your tempo, and make an appointment for some time with an instructor on the range. Work on changing your mind before you start changing your swing.

73

SAY UNCLE

There are days on the golf course when nothing seems to be going right (or when every-thing's going too far right). What to do about it? You've tried all your swing keys, setup techniques, and mind-calming mantras. At a certain point you have to say "Uncle!"—give in and just acknowledge that this is one of those days that isn't going your way. Just giving up the struggle can be enough to free you up to make a couple of good swings, and maybe even salve your wounds by playing a couple of holes well.

Give up on posting a good score. Remember, the handicap system throws out the highest ten scores of your last twenty rounds, so this one won't count anyway.

Have some fun trying hero shots—you'll have plenty of opportunities because you're already hitting into places that require heroic recoveries.

Finally, have a sense of humor about your pre-dicament instead of beating yourself up. After all, isn't where you have to play it from punishment enough?

"A positive outlook and never-give-up attitude both require total belief in yourself and the ability to live with the outcome, whether good or bad."

Tiger Woods

Getting of Troub

A. Ravielli

74

BE PREPARED TO SCRAMBLE

A round of golf can turn around in the blink of an eye. When we hit a great shot, our confidence soars and we feel as though we're on the right track. However, when we hit a bad shot, we can lose our nerve, and with it goes the commitment necessary to allow our best swings to come through.

If you are skilled in playing recovery shots, you'll feel more confident about handling a wider variety of results. Therefore, one way to reduce the fear of unwanted results is to strengthen your short game and capability to recover from wayward shots.

When you miss a green, don't hang your head and lament a missed opportunity for a birdie. Take the attitude that you now will get to demonstrate how good your short game is.

75

GET IT BACK INTO PLAY

When we find our ball in a trouble spot on the golf course, our first thought is about how to recover. We want to get the most out of our recovery shot, but we also need to be realistic and not try a shot that will leave us in as bad a position, or one that's even worse.

There are three priorities in deciding on the shot to play: out, on, and close. First, be sure that the shots you're considering will get you *out* of the trouble you're in (and not into more trouble). If you have confidence in a shot that will get you out of trouble, the next priority is getting *on* the fairway or green. Don't force a shot trying to get closer to the hole that leaves you in the rough or in a bunker. Only if you are sure you can get out and on should you play a shot trying to get the ball *close*.

Stick to the order of *out*, *on*, and *close* in choosing your recovery shots and you'll play smarter and shoot lower scores.

A. Ravielli

76

TWEENERS

When you find yourself between clubs on a shot, going with your gut feeling will serve you better than basing your choice on complicated calculations. Set up to the shot with each club, feeling the level of tension in your body with each. If one club makes you feel uneasy and the other gives you a feeling of comfort and relief, your body is telling you which club you'll swing with more confidence. Trust your intuition and pick the one that puts your mind and body at ease.

77 DOWNHILL LIES

As human beings, we are hardwired to avoid falling down. When faced with a downhill lie, or a sidehill lie with the ball below our feet, the instinct to maintain our balance actually works against us. Instead of swinging down along the contour of the ground, we instinctively shift backward onto our heels to maintain our balance, causing a scoop or a flip of the club through impact. That's why we often hit thin shots from a downhill lie, and why the shot we expect to fade or slice because the ball is below our feet turns out to be a pull or a hook.

The remedy is to swing as if you intend to *let yourself fall* as you follow through, but be ready to step through with your back foot to catch yourself and keep from actually falling down. Gary Player was a master at doing so, and even did that step-through move on level shots for a bit of extra power.

78

PLAY FROM A FAIRWAY BUNKER

The problem most people have with this shot stems from trying to pick the ball clean and at the same time trying to help it into the air. That practically guarantees hitting it thin, right into the lip of the bunker. Some people swing as if they're in a greenside bunker, hitting the sand well behind the ball, advancing it only a few yards. Either result is understandably frustrating.

Here's an image that will let you make the simplest, most effective swing from a fairway bunker.

First, set up with the ball an inch farther back in your stance than you would for a normal shot with the same club. That gives you a better chance of contacting the ball first.

Second, keep in mind that if you were in the fairway, you'd want to make contact with the ball before the grass, so why play this shot any differently? Imagine as vividly as you can that the ball is sitting on the short grass of a closely mown fairway. Then swing away just as you would from the fairway. The more vivid and convincing your image of the ball sitting on grass, the easier it will be to swing in an ordinary way. You'll be amazed at how easy it is to play from a fairway bunker with this image in mind.

79

CLEARING THE LIP

Golfers waste shots when they try to play a long iron from a fairway bunker and hit the lip in front of them, leaving the ball in the bunker. When you have to clear the lip of a bunker, your first priority should be to take a club with enough loft to allow the shot to get over the lip—even if that club won't get you all the way to the green.

The mental consequence of not being sure you are playing enough loft is a lack of confidence and commitment when swinging that club. That can make you try to help the ball into the air, resulting either in a thin shot into the lip or a fat shot that only goes a few yards.

To have confidence that the club you are choosing has enough loft, hold the club just above the surface of the sand near your ball, with the *back* of the clubhead facing downward, the *face* of the club pointing straight upward, and the *shaft* in line with the direction of the shot you want to play. If the shaft points into the lip or below it, you need to use a club with more loft. If the shaft points above the lip of the bunker, you can be certain that the club will have enough loft to clear the lip with an ordinary swing and play the shot with confidence.

80

AWKWARD STANCES

When you have an unusual or awkward stance for a golf shot, the unfamiliar feeling can distract you from your focus on executing the swing you need to make. The more familiar you get with the feeling of your stance and the angle of your swing, the more comfortable you'll be playing the shot.

Take the club you intend to swing, and assume the stance you intend to take. Waggle the club a bit, feeling what it will be like to swing from that position. Let your body get used to the way that stance feels. Say to yourself, "This is how it will feel when I actually make my swing." Now go back and start your full routine.

When you retake your stance, it will already seem more familiar and comfortable, and will be less of a distraction. You'll be more focused on executing the shot, and you'll have a better chance of success in doing so.

81

DEEP GRASS BY THE GREEN

Here's the challenge: You're in deep grass near the green. The ball is sitting down below the top of the grass. You don't have a long stretch of green between you and the hole.

Typically, you'd play the ball well back in your stance, trying to hit steeply downward so as to hit the back of the ball without the grass being in the way. However, it will be impossible not to have some grass get between the clubface and the ball, eliminating spin, and playing the ball back reduces the effective loft of the club. The result will be a low, running shot that goes zooming by the pin, leaving you with a very long putt to save par.

Try this other approach: Imagine that the ball is sitting in a greenside bunker and play the shot the way you would in that situation. With the ball forward in your stance, hold your lob wedge or sand wedge with the face open. Swing into the grass a couple of inches *behind* the ball, following through under the ball and into the same finish you would for a bunker shot. The ball will float out on the pile of grass you've dug out, landing softly on the green.

82

TWO HANDFULS OF SAND

Many players aren't sure how big a swing to make to send their greenside bunker shots the distance they want, especially when there's a good length of green to carry. Here's a mental image that has produced good results for many of my students, from high handicappers to professionals.

Picture the ball sitting in the middle of two handfuls of sand, in a shallow bowl made with open palms, fingers held together and curved slightly upward. Imagine how much sand that is, and how big a swing you'd need to make to send that amount of sand flying all the way to the hole. Get a feel for this in a practice bunker by actually scooping up two handfuls of sand and tossing them underhand into the air toward a hole.

The image of sending two handfuls of sand flying toward the hole also promotes a good, aggressive swing through the sand beneath the ball. Deceleration at impact is a common problem for many golfers, and swinging with this image in mind eliminates that fault.

Try this technique and see how much better your distance control is on greenside bunker shots.

83

ADD MORE NOISE

As quiet as we'd like it to be when we're about to swing, that's not always under our control. Sometimes there is a loud group in the next fairway, construction on a house bordering the course, or maintenance workers driving mowers nearby. It's easy for your mind to dwell on or anticipate a sound, and to lose focus on the feel of the swing or the image of the target.

Here's a surprise for you. It works better to *add* more sound than trying to block out sound. A pitcher in a major league baseball park might have 50,000 fans screaming at him, but he can't hear any of them because it all becomes a sort of "white noise" with no sudden, distracting burst of sound identifiable above the din.

On the course, if you stand over your ball wondering when the next mower will start, try to imagine the roar of the crowd in a stadium absorbing any sounds, and play your shot with the confidence that you won't be distracted in mid-swing.

84. KEEP YOUR CHIN UP

Our states of mind affect our bodies. When we are feeling down or upset mentally, our bodies feel clunky and unsettled. When we are happy and confident, our bodies feel comfortable and full of pep.

You can tell which golfers are playing well and which are struggling by the way they walk as they play their last few holes.

Conversely, our bodies also affect our states of mind. When you walk with your head down and your shoulders slumped, your mind takes its cue and figures that things are going poorly. You lose confidence and things get even worse. But it doesn't have to be that way.

Even if you've been playing poorly, walk to your next shot with a positive posture: chin up, shoulders back. Being aware of yourself in that good posture will help you feel more confident, and that will give you the best chance of turning things around.

85

STICK TO YOUR GAME PLAN

If you find yourself behind in a tournament, don't try to make up lost strokes from earlier holes by going away from your game plan. You may think about using your driver on a short, tight hole for which you had planned to use an iron or hybrid off the tee. Or you might shoot at a tucked pin when you had planned to play for the middle of the green. Taking unnecessary risks may get you out of the frying pan, but more likely you'll land in the fire.

You can't win the tournament on the front nine, but you can go a long way toward losing it if you aren't smart. In the long run, your odds of catching up are better if you stick to your game plan.

"Hit the putt as well as you can, and do not allow worry over the outcome to spoil the stroke."
Bobby Jones

Holing C

ıt

86

MAKE EVERY PUTT

Jack Nicklaus once commented that he had never missed a crucial putt on the last hole of a tournament. When someone in the audience reminded him of a particular situation in which he had missed, Nicklaus replied, "I didn't miss the putt. The ball missed the hole."

That's an important distinction. Let's call your job *making* the putt, which means executing the putt you intend. If it goes in, we'll call that *holing* the putt.

The language you use, even in your thinking, is very important. If you are trying to judge the *perfect* line and the *perfect* pace, there are many ways to get it wrong. By making your task simply to choose the best path and pace that you can, you can't miss.

If you chose the best path, used your best feel for pace, and made the best stroke that you could, you made your putt.

You may not hole every putt, but you can make every putt. Playing with the feeling that you can make any putt does wonders for your confidence. In putting, confidence makes all the difference in the world.

87

DON'T YOU WORRY

Some tour pros say that they putt their best when they don't care if they miss. It's hard to believe they don't care when they are playing for a small fortune at every tournament. What they actually mean by not *caring* is not *worrying*. It's natural to care about holing your putt. The point is not to worry about whether or not you will hole it.

Pretending not to care about a shot is a mistaken approach that usually produces a loose and sloppy swing—and a poor result. Don't kid yourself. Of course you care—if you didn't, you wouldn't be playing golf. But you can care without worrying. If you care in the right way, you'll be focused and committed to your process, without anxiety about the outcome.

You will putt your best by committing to your judgment of the path and pace of the putt, setting up and flowing into the stroke without a moment of hesitation. As Bobby Jones said, "Hit the putt as well as you can, and do not allow worry over the outcome to spoil the stroke."

Trust your routine and there's a much better chance that your stroke will be smooth and steady. If you're free from worry about whether or not the putt will go in, you'll find that it goes in more often.

88

ARE THE GREENS AS FAST AS THEY LOOK?

Here's a way to get a feel for the pace of the greens even before you start your warm-up. As you approach the practice green, guess how fast or slow the green looks to you in comparison to other greens that you've putted on before. Then roll two or three golf balls from the fringe to an open area of the green, away from any particular hole.

As you roll the balls on, you'll have an expectation of when they're likely to come to a stop, based on your sense of the speed of the green. If they stop sooner, you'll realize that the green is slower than it looks. If they keep on rolling past the point at which you expected them to stop, you'll know that the green is faster than it looks.

If you squat down at the edge of the green, you can get a worm's-eye view of how the balls roll, noticing how bumpy or smooth the green is and how the ball reacts if the green is grainy. That's helpful because you see each ball roll and feel it directly from your hand rather than through the putter.

Take all this information with you to the course and you'll quickly develop a good feel for the speed of the greens.

89

PUTTING WARM-UP

When you start your putting warm-up before a round, begin by "putting to nowhere." Since there's no hole, you'll make your natural stroke without pushing or pulling the putt toward the hole. Work on this until you feel like you're hitting it on the sweet spot every time and your putts are rolling end over end.

Next roll some long putts to get a feel for how big a swing you need to make to get them to travel the correct distance.

Then try some medium-length putts to holes on side slopes to get a feel for the relationship of pace to break. Experiment with a variety of speeds and paths for each putt.

Finish your putting warm-up with several two-foot putts, focusing primarily on keeping your head steady and listening for each putt landing in the hole. The stroke is virtually identical to the one you'll use for putts of four or five feet. And you'll hear the ball rattling into the bottom of the cup—the sound of success that builds confidence.

90 READING A PUTT

To read your putt, start from a wide view. Look at the overall lay of the land and, within that, the general slope of the green. Modern architects take drainage into account in their design, so look for the low spot on the border of the green where water is intended to run off. Determine if there is grain in the grass that will affect your putt.

After that, shift to a narrower focus. Look for the sidehill, uphill, or downhill slopes between the ball and the hole, including the subtle undulations that will influence the direction or pace of the ball as it rolls.

Look especially at the last few feet near the hole. That's where your ball will be moving most slowly, and therefore where gravity and grain will have the most effect. Find the spot on the edge of the hole that you expect the ball to go over, and choose the pace at which you'd like it to be rolling as it drops in.

Based on what you saw, trace backward from the hole to the ball along the imagined path that you judge the ball needs to take to enter the hole on the spot and at the pace you intend. You want to choose the path and the pace that will give you the best chance of holing the first putt without leaving you a long second one.

a. Ravielli

91

USE YOUR FEET AS WELL AS YOUR EYES

In reading a putt, it's news to many golfers that they can use their feet as well as their eyes. Walk along (but not directly on) the area of the green between your ball and the hole. Some people find it helpful to walk first on one side of the putt and then back on the other. Put as much of your awareness as you can into your feet and your sense of balance. Feel how much or how little the slope of the ground tilts you to one side or the other, and how much you sense that you're walking uphill, downhill, or on level ground.

Merge what your feet are telling you with what your eyes are seeing. Sometimes our eyes can play tricks on us, so if in doubt, you may want to put your faith in your feet instead.

92

PLAY FOR MAXIMUM BREAK

For putts that will travel across a slope of the green, play for maximum break. As Bobby Jones said, "It is always a good practice to borrow generously from any slope and attempt to cause the ball to pass a tiny bit above the hole. There is always a chance it will fall into the upper side, and it is certain that it will stop not far away. But once a putt begins to roll below the hole, every inch it travels carries it farther from that precious cup."

On the practice green, try different paths on which to play a breaking putt until you find the maximum amount of break and still have the ball reach the hole. It won't be going very fast as it gets there, so if it misses it won't roll too far by.

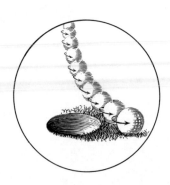

Putts that have a lot of break require that you only concern yourself with the first half of the putt. You have to roll the ball up the hill just far enough to get the ball in position for gravity to pull it down the slope in the second half of the putt on the way to the hole.

93

HAVE A RELIABLE PUTTING ROUTINE

Read your putt and make a strong commitment to the path and pace you've chosen. Stand a few paces behind the ball, looking down your visualized path. Some people take a practice stroke or two at this point, facing down the path.

Take a full breath, and settle into your body as you complete your exhalation.

Feel the ground with your feet as you walk slowly forward and turn toward the ball. Some people take a practice stroke or two at this point, just to the side of the ball, facing parallel to the path.

Set the putterhead behind the ball, facing down the start of the path, holding the putter with a soft grip. Then set your stance.

Look along your path from the ball to the hole, and reaffirm your commitment to that path. If you feel any doubt, step back for another look.

Soften your gaze, relax your arms, and let the putter swing smoothly through impact along the path. Hold the finish of your stroke for a few seconds. While keeping your posture stable, turn your head to look as the ball rolls down the path, hopefully into the hole.

94

EVERY PUTT IS STRAIGHT

I tell my students that every putt is a straight putt. It's important to understand that I don't mean that literally, but simply that at the start of every putt you should stroke the ball as if you were rolling a straight putt. Swing straight down the path on which you aim the putter, perpendicular to the putter-face. This makes your putting more consistent; you never need to push or pull a putt for more or less break. The only variable in the execution of a putt is the size of your stroke.

The point is to stroke every putt that way, aiming for the break you see, letting gravity and the contours of the green move the ball in one direction or another as it rolls toward the hole. See what happens and learn from it for reading future putts—but always stroke them straight.

95

HOLD THE PUTTER LIGHTLY

When you hold the putter lightly and maintain that same amount of pressure throughout the stroke, it's less likely that you will guide or direct the putt. If you are just rotating your shoulders with steady posture, there can't be any pushing or pulling. This is how you putt when you're practicing your stroke. If you pay attention, you'll notice that when you do alter the path of the putterhead as you swing, you will have tightened your grip to do so.

Sam Snead liked to say that your grip should have the same pressure you'd use if you were holding a small bird just firmly enough not to let it fly away. To maintain a soft, consistent pressure throughout his stroke, Jack Nicklaus imagined that the shaft of his putter was like the delicate stem of a wine glass that would snap if his grip tightened at all during the stroke. Those are good images to give you the feel of holding the putter lightly throughout your stroke.

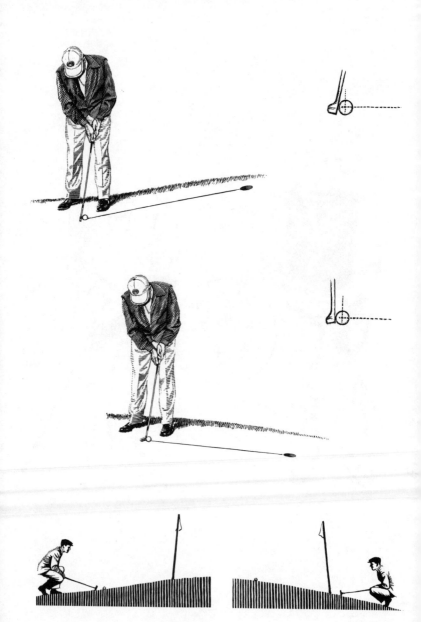

96

WATCH YOUR SPEED

Distance is the most critical factor in successfully executing long putts. Focus on an image of the pace at which the putt will enter the hole. That will give you greater precision in getting a feel for the distance.

On an uphill putt, imagine the ball popping into the back of the hole. This encourages you to stroke the ball firmly, without needing to intentionally make an extra-hard stroke. For level putts, picture the ball pouring into the hole. On a downhill putt, imagine the ball just trickling over the front edge. This encourages you to stroke the ball softly, but not so tentatively that you leave it short.

A common technique for long putts is to putt toward an imaginary circle with a six-foot diameter around the hole. The problem with this technique is having too big a target—it's easy to lose focus and make too casual a stroke.

Instead, picture the ball actually going into the hole, even on long putts. Make the best read you can, and give the ball the best roll you can. If it doesn't go in, your misses will end up closer to the hole. That means fewer three-putts and lower scores.

97

MAKE THAT COMEBACKER

After their first putt travels well past the hole, many golfers leave the comebacker short. If that's the case for you, this tip will help.

In your mind, you don't want the ball to go too far past the hole again and risk an embarrassing *four-putt*. That makes you tighten up, become very cautious, and maybe even decelerate as you stroke the second putt. More than likely, it doesn't reach the hole. And there has never been a putt that fell in without reaching the hole.

When you face a comebacker, don't think about what will happen if you miss. Focus instead on following your regular routine as if this were your first putt. To counter the tendency to be cautious, simply pick a point on the back edge of the cup and make that your target. You'll have a better chance of getting the second putt all the way to the hole, and that's the only way it has a chance of going in.

98

SHOULD YOU PUTT OR CHIP?

The situation: The ball is on the fringe, just a few feet off the green. Should you putt or chip?

You might want to know the rule of thumb used by the pros. If they are trying to hole it, they chip; if they just want to get down in two, they putt.

The following classic tip explains the smartest choice for the average player. Arnold Palmer pointed out to a young Jack Nicklaus that the worst result you would expect from a putt is about the same as a good result from a chip, so he usually chose the putter.

Unless you're a low handicapper intending to chip it in, choose the putter like Arnold did.

99

POST-PUTT ROUTINE

Having a post-putt routine will improve both your ability to read greens and your ability to stroke putts with confidence.

If you made the putt you intended, give yourself a mental pat on the back by saying, "That's just the way I felt the pace would be and how I saw the break." That builds confidence by reinforcing your successful process of reading and stroking the putt.

If the pace wasn't quite right, stand to the side and see if there was something in the slope or grain of the green that caused you to misjudge the pace. Then go back to the spot you putted from and make an adjusted practice stroke, based on how the last putt turned out. Make that stroke bigger or smaller, such that it would roll the ball the correct distance.

If the putt broke differently than you expected, look at the lay of the land, the overall slope of the green, and the area that you putted across to discover one of two things: what you didn't see that affected the putt or what you saw that you thought would affect the putt but didn't. Picture the path that would have been more correct.

Every time you go through this routine you'll refine your eye for reading putts and gauging speed, and you'll gain more confidence in the stroke, path, and pace you choose for your next putt.

100

PUTTING IS A GUESSING GAME

Putting is a guessing game. You don't know exactly how gravity or the grass surface will affect the ball. You make your best guess of the combination of path and pace, put your best stroke on it, and see what happens.

When reading a putt, the order to follow in judging path and pace isn't set in stone. You may first get a sense of how fast the ball needs to roll to reach the hole, then an idea of how far to the right or left it needs to travel for it to ride the slope toward the hole. That view may change your sense of pace: for example, you may need to start the putt going faster to get far enough up the slope for it to then turn and roll down again toward the hole.

Practice by testing a variety of paths for a breaking putt. Play it as firmly as you dare, with little break, then try other paths that require less pace but more break, until you play the maximum amount of break and the softest pace at which the ball will still make it all the way to the hole. That way you will discover the most comfortable combination for you.

Being more comfortable makes it easier to commit to your read, allowing you to make a more confident stroke. And nothing is more important in golf than confidence.

First published in the
United States of America in 2009
by Universe Publishing
A Division of Rizzoli International Publications, Inc.
300 Park Avenue South
New York, NY 10010
www.rizzoliusa.com

2009 2010 2011 2012 / 10 9 8 7 6 5 4 3 2 1

Design by Opto

Printed in the United States

ISBN-13: 978-0-7893-1865-7

Library of Congress Catalog Control Number: 2008910972

Neither the publisher nor the author is engaged in rendering professional advice or
services to the individual reader. Physical activity may result in injury if done
improperly or if not suitable for your particular physical condition. Accordingly,
before beginning any exercise regimen, or if you feel pain or discomfort while
exercising, it is recommended that you consult your healthcare professional.
Neither the author nor the publisher shall be liable or responsible for any loss or
damage allegedly arising from any information or suggestion in this book.